GALAXY OF SUPERSTARS

CHELSEA HOUSE PUBLISHERS

GALAXY OF SUPERSTARS

Aerosmith

Erik Anjou

CHELSEA HOUSE PUBLISHERS
Philadelphia

Frontis: The "Toxic Twins" of Aerosmith, guitarist Joe Perry and singer Steven Tyler, perform at the "United We Stand: What More Can I Give?" benefit concert held on Sunday, October 21, 2001 at RFK Stadium in Washington, DC.

CHELSEA HOUSE PUBLISHERS
Editor in Chief: Sally Cheney
Director of Production: Kim Shinners
Creative Manager: Takeshi Takahashi
Manufacturing Manager: Diann Grasse

Staff for AEROSMITH
Associate Editor: Ben Kim
Picture Researcher: Jane Sanders
Production Assistant: Jaimie Winkler
Series Designer: Takeshi Takahashi
Cover Designer: Terry Mallon
Layout: 21st Century Publishing and Communications, Inc.

The Chelsea House World Wide Web address is
http://www.chelseahouse.com

First Printing

1 3 5 7 9 8 6 4 2

Library of Congress Cataloging-in-Publication Data

Anjou, Erik.
    Aerosmith / by Erik Anjou.
       p. cm. — (Galaxy of superstars)
Summary: Profiles Aerosmith, the rock group whose string of hits, which has spanned over twenty-five years, includes "Dream On," "Walk this Way," and "Draw the Line."
Includes bibliographical references (p.   ) and index.
    ISBN 0-7910-6771-8 (hardcover)
  1. Aerosmith (Musical group)—Juvenile literature. 2. Rock musicians—United States—Biography—Juvenile literature. [1. Aerosmith (Musical group) 2. Musicians. 3. Rock music.] I. Title. II. Series.
ML3930.A17 A5 2002
782.42166'092'2—dc21
                                                                    2002000988

CONTENTS

1

NINE LIVES

I t was a Tuesday night in 1998 at the Pepsi Arena in Albany, New York. The hard-hitting rock and roll quintet Aerosmith was nearing the end of a fiery rendition of its recent Top 20 hit, "Draw the Line." Lead guitarist Joe Perry dropped suddenly and dramatically to his knees. And as the song's last notes ached from his guitar, he toppled over onto the stage, seemingly lifeless. Perry stayed on the ground, not moving, for what seemed like ages. His body was frozen in a pale blue spotlight. Then Perry shot back up to his feet, re-slung his guitar, and ripped into a savage reprise of the song. The audience howled its approval. Aerosmith was back from the dead and rocking.

Aerosmith consists of five members: lead singer Steven Tyler, lead guitarist Joe Perry, rhythm guitarist Brad Whitford, bassist Tom Hamilton, and drummer Joey Kramer. Steven was born in 1948, and Joe was born in 1950. Brad, the youngest member of the band, was born in 1952. By the time the musicians were treating the sold-out Pepsi Arena crowd to a glorious rock 'n' roll extravaganza, the legendary group had been in business for nearly 27 years. Steven and Joe were old enough to be most of the audience members' parents. And yet, under the power of the spellbinding lights and hard-driving anthems, the years seemed to melt away. For Aerosmith, it was

Steven Tyler's trademark scarf on the microphone is one of many familiar things about the band Aerosmith.

a dream come true. It was all, finally, just about the music.

The story of Aerosmith's rise to glory in the 1970s, its fall from grace, and its eventual return to the mountain top is as famous (or infamous) as classic songs like "Dream On," "Walk This Way," and "Sweet Emotion." The band formed in 1970, and its debut was at a homecoming concert at Nimpoc Regional High School in Hopkinton, Massachusetts. Five years later, Aerosmith was poised to go into the recording studio with Columbia Records to produce its groundbreaking third album, *Toys in the Attic*. The album catapulted the band to national attention and musical stardom. But it also served to highlight the beginning of two dangerous and destructive cycles—first, Steven Tyler and Joe Perry's drug abuse, and second, the fierce, bitter arguments that started to erode the pair's once ironclad friendship. These cycles eventually led to the disintegration of the original group in 1979. Joe Perry later commented, "Back when we started, there was never any talk of doing this past 30. Many died before they hit that age—live for today, have a good time. They asked Ringo what he was going to do when the Beatles broke up in two years, and he said, 'Buy a hairdressing salon and be a barber.' The mentality was, it's never going to last. It takes a lot of work to do it."

The lifespan of Aerosmith is remarkable not only because of its length, but because it also helps to illustrate the evolution of rock and roll, heavy metal, and pop music in America. The 1960s—when Steven and Joe were both entering their mid-teens—was the era of the Beatles and the British invasion. The Beatles, sometimes called The Fab Four, first touched down in the United States on February 7, 1964. The 73 million people who watched their subsequent appearance on the Ed Sullivan television show were a testament to the group's extraordinary popularity and influence. Joe said it was the Beatles who first motivated him to play the electric guitar. Bassist Tom Hamilton was also a devoted Beatlemaniac. His high school band, in keeping with the bug theme, was named the Mosquitos.

The Beatles were joined by the Rolling Stones, the Animals, the Yardbirds, and many more. And as the 1960s unfolded and evolved, so did the sound of rock and roll—and especially that of the electric guitar. The guitar's sound took on as many different nuances as its diverse, increasingly experimental players, and its range encompassed the beautiful, melodic twang of the early Beatles, the driving, rhythm and blues groove of the Rolling Stones, and the guttural, heavy metal aggression of Led Zeppelin and Jimi Hendrix. The five teenagers who were to become Aerosmith grew up in the midst of this revolutionary wave of sound. As a matter of fact, one of Steven's early bands, Chain Reaction, actually opened in 1968 for the soon-to-be-defunct Yardbirds. (The Yard-birds then featured the extraordinary guitarist Jimmy Page, who would forge more rock history with Led Zeppelin.)

There was another more intangible—and potentially dangerous—element that accompanied rock and roll: the lifestyle. In the documentary film *The Decline of Western Civilization: The Heavy Metal Years*, Motorhead member Lemmy states, "If your parents don't like it, it's good." The idea of rebellion is central to rock and roll music. And whereas singer-songwriters such as Bob Dylan and Crosby, Stills, Nash & Young also helped make social justice and political consciousness a critical ingredient, the wild image of rock remained a large part of its message. Rock 'n' roll music embodied a cry against the norm and often endorsed a non-conformist, in-your-face attitude.

The 1960s were a time of monumental change in the United States. The years bore witness to the assassinations of President John F. Kennedy, his brother Robert, and Martin Luther King, Jr. in addition to the escalation of the Vietnam War. The sound of rock and roll came to echo the turmoil of society itself, as did the unconventional, wild lifestyle that surrounded it. Steven loved it when visiting English bands toured the Northeast United States. He would stand outside a group's hotel just to catch a glimpse of them. For Steven and his young bandmates, there was nothing more impressive than being a rock star; to look like a rocker looked, to do what he did. The prominent role that drugs and alcohol often played in the rock and roll culture would haunt the members of Aerosmith for many years to come.

In the spring of 1984, the original members of Aerosmith reunited after a separation of nearly five years. With a new dedication to each other, to sobriety, and to the integrity of their music, Aerosmith launched themselves anew. In 1986 the group contributed to Run-DMC's dynamic rap reworking of "Walk This Way." The single reached the No. 4 spot on the Billboard chart, and the accompanying music video helped catapult Aerosmith back into national prominence.

But the band didn't stop there. In 1996 the Boston Music Awards named Aerosmith the band of the decade—even though there were four more years left until 2000. And nothing in the group's wildest imagination could have prepared it for the bonanza of 1998. Aerosmith contributed a handful of songs (including "I Don't Want to Miss a Thing")

to the movie soundtrack of the Jerry Bruckheimer-produced *Armageddon*. When the dust finally cleared, *Armageddon* finished as Hollywood's top-grossing film of 1998 (earning $202 million), "I Don't Want to Miss a Thing" became Aerosmith's first-ever number one hit, and the song's music video won an MTV Video Music Award. Aerosmith was invited to the White House. Minnesota Governor-elect Jesse "The Body" Ventura asked the band to play at his 1999 inauguration. And Aerosmith was given VIP status at Cape Canaveral, where they watched the *Discovery* launch that put US Senator John Glenn back into space.

Perhaps it's the idea of space itself that best defines the band. If John Glenn can revisit zero-gravity after thirty-five years, then why can't a drug-free, dedicated Aerosmith continue its rollicking, high-octane rock and roll adventure well into the 21st century? Steven Tyler concurs. "I think it's interesting," he says, "we're finally coming full circle."

Aerosmith's new status as a pop and rock icon brought new opportunities. A firm relationship with MTV netted Aerosmith a Super Bowl appearance. The guys, all near 50 years old, performed their latest hit with Britney Spears and 'NSync, rockers who are less than half Aerosmith's age.

2

THE HEART OF
ROCK AND ROLL

Steven Tyler was born Steven Tallarico on March 26, 1948. Music lived within the walls of the Tallarico's middle-class home. Steven's father, Victor, was a Julliard-trained classical pianist. The elder Tallarico had performed at Carnegie Hall, and taught music in the New York City public schools. Victor's grandfather (Steven's great-grandfather) was a cellist, a chamber musician who had played in some of New York's fanciest hotel ballrooms. Victor was a quiet man, and not overly communicative or verbal as a father. Says Steven, "My father talked to me with his fingers, playing Debussy and Beethoven." He adds, "I grew up under the piano."

Steven attended Roosevelt High School in Yonkers, New York. The teenager was appreciated more for his rebellious, mischievous streak than for his grades. A smart, creative teenager, he was also undisciplined and displayed a definite wild streak. Steven was often beaten up by his bigger peers (who made fun of his lips), and he later joined a gang called the Green Mountain Boys. He experimented with marijuana and other substances and was eventually thrown out of Roosevelt. The dramatic climax came when a police car pulled up in front of the Tallarico house and the authorities

Steven Tyler signing a copy of the Aerosmith autobiography *Walk This Way*. He was the first member to have entered the music business, already having made a record by the time he met the other future members of Aerosmith.

handcuffed Steven in front of his parents. One of the Green Mountain Boys' new running mates, it seemed, was actually an undercover Putnam County deputy sheriff.

The judge ultimately reduced the criminal charges, and Steven walked away with a misdemeanor. He was expelled from Roosevelt and returned to school at Quintano's, a private institution for creative, undisciplined teens. Unfortunately, Qunitano's turned out to be as undisciplined as its students. Steven never received much of a formal education. He later claimed to have skipped classes two days out of five.

Steven's real education was music, and in this sense the young man was extremely fortunate. The Tallarico family owned and operated Trow-Rico Lodge, a 360-acre resort in rural Sunapee, New Hampshire, and it was here where Steven spent his summers. The small town of Sunapee would turn out to be a fateful junction for Aerosmith. But for the time being, it was a place where Steven could exercise his creative and dramatic skills. He performed in comedy skits in the lodge's talent shows. He also began to join his father's swing band as a drummer. The band played regularly at the nearby upscale Sunapee Lodge.

The Beatles broke like a mighty wave across America in the early 1960s, and Steven—like many of his peers—was caught up in their tow. In 1964 Steven formed a band named The Strangeurs, a straightforward cover band that played the hit songs of the Beatles, the Rolling Stones, the Animals, and the Yardbirds. The Strangeurs soon changed their name to Chain Reaction, and they were regulars on the New York and New England club circuit. Steven also tried his hand at writing some original material for the band, but the singles weren't successful.

Steven's 1966 composition "When I Needed You" ended up resurfacing on Aerosmith's 1991 retrospective, *Pandora's Box*. Commented Steven 25 years after penning it, " [I]t's a pretty lame song. I never got a cent."

New York's Greenwich Village also became a popular second home for Steven in his raucous teenage years. He would take the train down from Westchester on a Friday afternoon and spend the night in the Village. He frequented the eateries and clubs that defined and embraced a new, rebellious generation of young Americans—Tin Angel, Night Owl, Bitter End, Bizarre, and Café Wha? Steven also fell in with the members of the band Left Banke. The group had produced a huge hit single, "Walk Away Renee," in 1967, but had been left floundering after the departure of its talented composer, Michael Brown. The

Steven Tyler, once teased for the size of his lips, became the face of Aerosmith. Tyler provided the lyrics for most of the band's hit songs as well as being the flamboyant frontman, although at first he thought he would play drums for the band. Here he poses with artist Peter Max who painted portraits of Tyler and had them shown in Boston.

ambitious Tallarico was given the opportunity to sing backup on two numbers on the group's subsequent 1968 album, *The Left Banke Too.*

The Left Banke made an important impression on Steven. He comments: "They had a hit under their belt, a million-seller nation-wide, and they were just the laziest [guys] ever. . . . I remember thinking, 'There's got to be a better way of doing this.' " Despite Steven's renewed dedication to his own Chain Reaction, the band began to fade. Chain Reaction had brief moments in the limelight—playing sporadic opening act spots for The Byrds, the Beach Boys, and the nearly defunct Yardbirds—but the band didn't have the hits or the acclaim they desired. Steven and his writing partner, Don Solomon, quit to form another new venture, William Proud. By the summer of 1969, however, William Proud was failing as well. The discouraged Steven packed his bags and left New York City, hitchhiking his way to his parents' place in Sunapee.

Joe Perry was born on September 10, 1950 in Lawrence, Massachusetts. His family was middle-class and intent on helping him pursue a background in classical music. Joe, however, had quite literally been bitten by the rock 'n' roll bug—also known as The Beatles. The Fab Four motivated him to start playing the electric guitar. He remembers: "When I was nine, I told my parents I wanted a guitar and they ended up buying me a Silvertone from Sears Roebuck for $14.95. . . . I'm left-handed and at first I tried to play it that way; then I realized I was playing it upside down. So I learned to play right-handed because the guitar book said to hold it that way."

Joe, like Steven, wasn't much of a student. Whereas Joe's parents convinced him to try a preparatory academy in lieu of the local high school, Joe eventually left school altogether. He told *Creem* magazine in 1980: "I can remember when I was working in the factory after dropping out of prep school. I'd wake up in the morning and I wouldn't drink any coffee or take any speed, I'd just put on Ten Years After's 'Goin' Home,' and I'd be up and moving for the rest of the day. Ever since, I've always wanted to do what they did."

Perry worked a frustrating minimum-wage factory job for two years before heading north to New Hampshire, where his parents owned a summer home. He worked several part-time jobs in and around Sunapee; one was as a dishwasher at an ice-cream parlor that Steven and Chain Reaction occasionally frequented. Joe also met and befriended Thomas William Hamilton, a rabid Beatlemaniac and aspiring bass guitarist. By 1966 the pair had formed the band, Pipe Dream. Pipe Dream eventually bloomed into a harder-edged, bluesy enterprise named Jam Band. The band's music was a combination of energy, loudness, and craziness. The group was apparently a little rough around the edges, but it did a passable job of covering hit singles by Cream, the Yardbirds, Ten Years After, and the MC5.

A small club, the Barn, was one of the hotspots in Sunapee. It was a simple country place. If you weren't old enough to drive there, you could simply scoot your 25 horsepower dinghy across the lake, tie up, and walk. The Jam Band was the Barn's house band, and the club's owner used to let Joe Perry sleep in an old farmhouse on the property. The cleaning lady would fix him eggs in the mornings. Meanwhile Steven Tallarico and Chain Reaction were already one of the venue's big draws. Joe recalls, "Steven sure looked like a rock star, and he *definitely* acted like one, so we just assumed he already was one."

The original line-up for Aerosmith, shown here in 1999. In the late '60s, it was Brad Whitford, Joey Kramer, Steven Tyler and Joe Perry who formed the core of Aerosmith (a name thought up by Joey Kramer) along with then-guitarist Steven Tabano.

One night, Tom Hamilton remembers trying to catch Steven's act at the Barn. The place was so crowded he couldn't even get inside. He says, "Steven had already put out a *record*, for God's sake. He was the real thing." One night Joe summoned the courage to invite Steven to a Jam Band show. And whereas Steven wasn't particularly impressed with the band's technique or tightness, he was won over by its sheer energy and commitment. Steven remembers, "I'd been playing in bands for something like seven years at this point. And we were always trying to get ahead, trying to rehearse and sound professional. But then I go to see the Jam Band, and it blew me away. . . . [T]hey got up there and did "Rattlesnake Shake" by Fleetwood Mac. And I said to myself, 'That's it. . . .' I just knew that if I could show them a little of what I knew, with the looseness and [determination] that they showed up there, then we'd really have something."

Tallarico, Perry, and Hamilton agreed to hook up. At first Steven wanted to double up on vocals and drums, displacing original Jam Band percussionist Pudge Scott. But he soon decided he would be more effective solely as lead singer and frontman. Steven also suggested using a second guitarist to help fill out the fledgling band's sound. His recommendation was Steven Tabano, a childhood buddy from Yonkers who had played in Steven's William Proud.

Tabano was at the time running an expensive leather goods store in Boston. He suggested that "Beantown" might be a good place for the new band to set up camp. Boston was also to become an important choice because it is where the band's new drummer-to-be, Joey Kramer, was living. Born in the Bronx, New York, in 1950, Kramer was studying at the acclaimed Berklee School of Music. But Berklee's focus was in classical studies, and Joey was eager to get back to rock and roll (he'd had previous experience with rock, soul, and R&B groups). One day Kramer popped by Ray Tabano's store to ask for an audition. Ironically, once he got the job he was hesitant to take it. Joey was more interested in the kind of rock forged by Jethro Tull and Jimi Hendrix. Ultimately, Steven Tallarico convinced him to stick with the unproven group.

It was a good omen. It was Kramer who would suggest the band's official name—Aerosmith—a moniker he had dreamed up back in high school.

3

SLOW RISE

"**W**e weren't too ambitious when we started out. We just wanted to be the biggest thing that ever walked the planet, the greatest rock band there ever was. We just wanted everything. We wanted it *all*," Steven Tyler said.

Joe Perry is more modest in his recollections: "I never envisioned what I was doing as part of a *career*. We just looked at the bands we idolized—like the Yardbirds—and we were blown away by how they could *play*. All we wanted to do was play like that, to be a great band like that."

Boston was in some ways a perfect place to settle in. It was a big city with a small town, historical feel. It was also, however, somewhat of a musical desert. The only two rock bands that were successfully operating there were the J. Geils Band and Modern Lovers; neither was exactly taking the music business by storm. Employment opportunities for a young band seemed limited to playing Top 40 covers for the university crowd. Additionally, these were tough financial times for the new quintet. The

---

Aerosmith in 1975. Their first two albums, *Aerosmith* and *Get Your Wings*, were big sellers in the Boston area, but received lukewarm response nationally. Still, their relentless touring schedule insured that more and more people would be exposed to their music through their high-energy live show.

five musicians shared an old, unkempt three-bedroom apartment on Commonwealth Avenue. They barely made a living doing odd jobs. For a while Tyler worked in a bakery. Perry was a janitor at a local synagogue. The band managed to procure a gratis rehearsal room at Boston University in exchange for playing for free at dances. Occasionally, the students would sneak the band members into the school cafeteria when they were desparate for food. "We ate a lot of brown rice back then," remembers Steven.

Aerosmith debuted in autumn of 1970 at Nimpoc Regional High School in Hopkinton, Massachusetts. The band blended many of their own compositions into a playlist that included the Rolling Stones, the Yardbirds, and John Lennon ("Cold Turkey"). An infamous Aerosmith tradition was instituted that evening; Steven and Joe Perry had a blowout argument about Joe playing too loudly. The fight was an emblem of the band's growing pains as it struggled to create a map for its future progress. Joey Kramer says, "[E]verybody had their own ideas about what they wanted the band to be. We came to realize that the one thing that we all had in common was that we all wanted to make it. And making it back then had nothing to do with being rich and famous. It had to do with being recognized, by your peers and people, for being a great band and being able to play concerts where a lot of people would come."

From the beginning, Aerosmith made a critical creative decision. They opted to perform only at venues where they could play their original songs—and to avoid the club and bar scene where the crowd expected to hear renditions of already well-known songs. The band considered itself to be a concert band, not a bar band, and its playing schedule shuffled the musicians to a diverse range of high school dances, fraternity parties, ski lodges, and even Navy officer's clubs. "Having to play four sets a night of other people's material really drains you," concludes Perry. "That's a trap a lot of young bands fall into—they get used to that $1,000 a week they're pulling in from playing at a club. It becomes hard for them to break out of that."

Aerosmith was working without a manager. The band had to rely on its own wits and self-promotional skills to develop a reputation outside of New England. There was also an increasing number of arguments about guitarist Steven Tabano's role in the enterprise. In 1971 Tabano left, disappearing to Mexico for several months. He eventually returned as Aerosmith's director of marketing, and was involved in designing the group's famous logo.

Brad Whitford was not only Tabano's replacement; he was the missing piece in the band's musical puzzle. Born in 1952 in Winchester, Massachusetts, Brad had received a deep and diverse musical education. As a teenager he studied trumpet before finally seizing upon the guitar. Later he spent a year studying music theory and composition at Berklee in Boston. Whitford provided Aerosmith with the perfect lush compliment to Perry's aggressive, electrifying guitar work.

When Brad joined Aerosmith the band was earning $300 a night. It was popular throughout southern New England but unknown anywhere else. The musicians had all quit their day jobs to devote themselves fully to their

music, and they were living hand-to-mouth. Fortunately, John O'Toole, the manager of Boston's Fenway Theater, came to the band's rescue. O'Toole had taken a liking to the group and allowed it to use the Fenway as free rehearsal space. One night he invited Frank Connolly, one of the city's most successful concert promoters, to hear them play. "Father Frank" signed on almost immediately. First, he helped the struggling musicians put their financial affairs in order. Second, he secured them a regular stint at the Manchester Sheraton Hotel. Aerosmith was now not only responsible for coming up with a number of new songs, it also got to live and rehearse at the hotel. Last but not least, Connolly engineered a deal with the savvy New York-based management duo, Steven Leber and David Krebs. Connolly knew that he would need Leber and Krebs's heavy-duty contacts in order to land the band a record deal.

It didn't take Leber and Krebs long to get things moving. After a showcase gig at the famous New York rock and roll dive, Max's Kansas City, the president of Columbia Records showed up backstage to tell the guys, "Yes, I think we could do something with you." Aerosmith signed with Columbia for $125,000 in the summer of 1972. By 21st century stan-dards, that's a small sum. But for a band that was teetering on the edge of poverty and running from eviction notices, the offer was manna from heaven. Aerosmith felt hot; stardom could only be just around the corner. The band couldn't get into Boston's Intermedia Sound to begin recording soon enough.

It took Aerosmith two weeks to lay down the eight tracks on its self-titled debut record,

Aerosmith replaced Steven Tabano with current guitarist Brad Whitford, shown here, whose rhythm guitar worked especially well with Joe Perry's leads.

Aerosmith. To this day, the album remains Brad Whitford's favorite. It embodies the brash, aggressive swagger of the band, its "in your face" energy and bluesy roots. One of the most important aspects of the record was Steven Tyler's (he had officially changed his name prior to the sessions) growing confidence as a songwriter. Songwriting wasn't the group as a whole's forte. Steven and Joe had written "Movin' Out" (based on an eviction notice at their Commonwealth Avenue apartment) years earlier. But "One Way Street," "Make It," "Write Me a Letter," and "Mama Kin" each evolved slowly, piece-by-piece. Oftentimes as the recording process progressed, the band members would literally be sleeping in their communal living room—and Steven would wake up, walk to the piano and start playing out an idea he'd had the night before. Seven of the eight tunes on *Aerosmith* were original compositions. Five were written by Steven, one by Steven and Steven Emspack, and one by Steven and Joe Perry. "Dream On" has not only become a rock classic; it has also been called the first-ever power ballad. *Aerosmith* additionally featured Steven's talent on the harmonica ("One Way Street") and the wood flute (Rufus Thomas's "Walkin' the Dog").

Steven was poised for immediate stardom. He was soon confronted, however, with the sobering realities of the music business. *Aerosmith* was released in January 1973—on the very same day as Bruce Springsteen's Columbia debut. For every $100 Columbia pumped into *Greetings from Asbury Park*, it spent $1 on *Aerosmith*. The Boston-area fans were of course rabid about the album, and "Dream On" quickly became the most-requested song on local rock stations. The tune never climbed higher than No. 59 on the Billboard national chart, however, and Columbia didn't release it as a single until June. The album's overall sales were disappointing, and the critics in particular came down hard on it. The consensus was, "They're like a K-Mart version of the Rolling Stones." This comparison would haunt Aerosmith for decades. To make matters worse, Leber and Krebs approached the band and issued a dire forecast: "Look, you know, I just talked to the record company and they said, 'Unless your next album is really, really good, you're not going to be recording artists anymore.'"

In the fall of 1973, Aerosmith entered New York's Record Plant to record its second album, *Get Your Wings*. The record was produced by Jack Douglas and Ray Colcord. Douglas soon proved to be invaluable. There was an immediate creative synchronicity between him and the band, and Jack became, according to Brad Whitford, "like our sixth member." The producer's challenge was to translate Aerosmith's brash, roguish qualities to the album itself. The attitude had to be in the music, not in the visual, physical posturing of the band.

Unfortunately there was one negative element to the recording sessions, a negative that was to take root and worsen. Steven was falling into alcohol and drug dependence. The actual cover of *Get Your Wings* in fact embodies both the band's swagger and its flirtation with danger. It features Steven wearing a scarf, a scarf he still owns to this day. He says, "Right about, oh four inches up, there was a little hole, and I would stuff it full of Tuinals. It's where I kept my drugs. That was my drug of choice: cocaine and a couple of Tuinals." Drugs were becoming a big part of his—and Joe Perry's—rock 'n' roll life.

Although *Get Your Wings* reflects a distinct growth in the band's developing sound and songwriting skills, its March 1974 release was met with the same general ambivalence as its first record. The album was again a top-seller in the Boston area, but couldn't crack the national consciousness. Aerosmith took to the road to promote it. The band was an opening act for both Black Sabbath and Deep Purple. It also headlined its own shows throughout New England and made its first national television appearance on NBC's *Midnight Special* on August 16. The experience was crucial in freeing Aerosmith to hone its stage act. Steven's physicality, high-test energy, and flamboyant costumes started to become a band trademark. He also began wearing his colorful, signature stage scarves.

Get Your Wings was never considered a hit. But thanks to the band's hard work and extensive touring, the album managed to stay around the middle of the charts. It sold a respectable 5,000 to 6,000 units per week and eventually went gold in 1975. Whatever excesses the band members were about to engage in, it was these early, unflagging efforts onstage and its no-nonsense, working-class connection to the fans that were digging a foundation for success. Aerosmith never strayed far from the audience's feeling of longing—of being fans on the other side of the rope. It's that spirit that infuses the band's meet-and-greet sessions with concert-goers to this very day. Joe states, "We were America's band. We were the garage band that made it really big—the ultimate party band. We were the guys you could actually see. Back then in the seventies it wasn't like Led Zeppelin was out there on the road in America all the time. The Stones weren't always coming to your town. We were. You could count on us to come by."

In early 1975, Aerosmith returned to the

Record Plant with producer Douglas to record its third album, *Toys in the Attic*. The band had been together for nearly four years. And whether it knew it or not, it was on the cusp of tasting Steven Tyler's ambitious declaration of having it all.

THE PEAK
AND THE VALLEY

4

"When you start a rock 'n' roll band," says Steven, "you've gotta fake it till you make it."

Aerosmith's *Toys in the Attic* was released in April 1975 and immediately burst into the *Billboard* Top 20. The album reached the gold record benchmark by the end of August, and went platinum by the end of the year. By the start of 1976 Aerosmith was Columbia Records' top-selling act. It had eclipsed Bruce Springsteen, Bob Dylan, and even Barbra Streisand. The new album's popularity prompted the re-release of "Dream On," which became Aerosmith's first Top 10 single. *Toys in the Attic* wound up selling more than five million copies.

One of the most commanding facets of the record was the tightened dynamic of the Tyler-Perry songwriting team. Steven either wrote or cowrote all eight of the album's original songs. The hit single "Walk This Way" sprung from a Perry guitar riff that he had ripped off during a sound check in Hawaii. Steven recalls that he wrote the song's lyrics the night before it was actually recorded; he had to scrawl the words on the walls of the Record Plant stairway so he could remember them. Hamilton adds that the number's title was borrowed from

---

Aerosmith started to get heavily involved with drugs when *Toys in the Attic* became successful, and the effects were becoming apparent.

a line in the film *Young Frankenstein*. It seems Jack Douglas had taken the band—minus Steven—to the movie to unwind after the day's recording session.

As the concert tour unfolded, Aerosmith began to emerge as a first-class rock and roll act, a kind of accidental bridge between the British sound of the 1960s and the unfolding decadence of the 1970s. There was nothing fancy or subtle about the band. It wrote about angst, about anger, and about sex. More than anything, Aerosmith dedicated itself to the fiery, blues-based soul of rock music. According to Steven, "The songs we write aren't the kind that you can come out and . . . genuflect. We play [outrageous] music." Joe however, was as concerned with the band's artistic essence as with its burgeoning stardom. He revealed, "Before, it was a struggle to keep alive. Now it's more of a struggle to find a sound. We can keep playing the largest arenas in the country, but we'd never be answering that question of our basic value. Our biggest struggle now is to make an artistic dent. General Motors makes a lot of money but doesn't have the respect of people who know cars."

The dark side of life in the limelight was also casting an ever-larger shadow. In June 1976, Steven and Joey Kramer were arrested in Lincoln, Nebraska, for staging an impromptu fireworks party in their hotel. In San Diego, Steven smashed the band's entire backstage buffet table. In Memphis, he was arrested at gunpoint for using profanity onstage. The police caught him as he tried to escape the theater lobby during a pre-encore blackout. The warning signs for an imminent meltdown were surfacing all over. But the band was on a roll—music, money, and popularity were the anointed priorities. Everything else could wait.

Aerosmith's controversial behavior continued as it entered the recording studio to produce its fourth album, *Rocks*. Steven was having a difficult time creating an album's worth of original lyrics. Whereas some of his lethargy could be attributed to the wear and tear of the preceding *Toys in the Attic* tour, it also emanated from his increased drug use. Steven's earlier experimentation had involved pot, barbiturates, and cocaine. But now he was using heroin regularly as well, as was partner Joe. Somehow, however, *Rocks* managed to be recorded with rock-hard intensity, a process held together by Jack Douglas. For many fans, the LP is considered *the* essential Aerosmith album, and its nine songs embodied the band's ever-tightening sound and musical sophistication. *Rocks* went platinum upon its 1976 release, and the band proceeded to spend two and a half months playing headliner shows in 10,000 seat plus arenas and outdoor stadiums. The 80,000 tickets for the show at the Silverdome in Pontiac, Michigan, sold out the day they went on sale. Aerosmith became one of the top-grossing U.S. concert acts, joining the esteemed ranks of Led Zeppelin, Alice Cooper, Jethro Tull, and Rod Stewart.

The quintet's spiraling popularity was matched by Steven's increased volatility and mood swings—aggravated, of course, by his worsening drug use. He became infamous for throwing temper tantrums, for blowing off interviews, and for arguing with Joe. In preparation for Aerosmith's upcoming United Kingdom tour, Leber and Krebs arranged an interview with an influential British journalist at Steven's recently purchased New Hampshire estate. Tyler hid out for two days in an empty building while the writer waited in his nearby mansion. Steven finally proceeded to give the journalist a tour of his land and gun collection. But he blew up at the writer when he declined to share the lines of cocaine Steven offered during the interview.

Ultimately, manager David Krebs had two choices. As the *Rocks* tour wound down, he could either push the band back into the studio as soon as possible to cut another album—or he could give them a break.

Aerosmith took several months off to relax during the first part of 1977. But whereas the free time certainly allowed the members to recuperate from the concert grind, it did little to diminish their detrimental behavior. When the group reconvened to record their next record, *Draw the Line*, it was in secluded Armonk in upstate New York, a safe distance from the temptations and distractions of New York City. Krebs dispatched Jack Douglas, the five musicians, and a massive amount of recording gear to a 300-room convent named The Centacle. The estate was virtually retooled as a combination recording studio-hotel.

The process was a disaster. Contrary to Krebs's intention, the Armonk locale provided its own license for excess, and much of the spring and summer of 1977 was spent waiting for Steven and Joe to get their acts together. Joe, it seems, had misplaced a demo tape on which he had laid down six tunes written specifically for the new album. Only now he was so drugged out he couldn't remember any of the songs. Steven, meanwhile, spent a significant portion of time locked up in the Centacle's tower with a shotgun trying to target the estate's assorted wildlife. Joey, Brad, and Tom would show up

every day at the rehearsal hall; Steven and Joe would limp in at night. Steven recalls, "We had motorcycles and Porsches and we'd go cruising around the countryside terrorizing everybody." Adds Perry: "The focus [was] completely gone. If I kept a journal, I couldn't do a better job of showing exactly where we went south. . . . The Beatles made their *White Album*; we made our Blackout Album."

When the record was finished, Tom Hamilton traveled to New Hampshire. He visited an old friend's house for a party and played the new cuts for everyone. Tom remembers, "[They] pretty much politely listened to it, and then I went up to my friend and I said, 'Wow, what do you think?' And he said, 'I think it sucks.'" All

Aerosmith in 1997 holding copies of the Aerosmith autobiography *Walk This Way*. After the release of *Toys in the Attic* the band began their descent into drug-fueled self-destruction, and it is a testament to their resilience and luck that they lived to tell the tale.

that diehard Aerosmith fans knew, however, was that a new record was due. When *Draw the Line* was released just before Christmas 1977, it quickly went platinum. The band's momentum increased again in 1978 with its onscreen roles in the Beatle-less film version of *Sgt. Pepper's Lonely Hearts Club Band.* Aerosmith's cover of "Come Together" emerged as a Top 20 hit.

The group's 1978 stadium concert tour was a mixed success. The good news was that the group continued to create and foster a genuine relationship with their fans. The bad news was that their erratic, often embarrassing comportment was becoming an inescapable obstacle to both their health and future success. The band could rarely be bothered to play sound checks before a show, and its performances were often lackluster, missing the vitality and aggression that defined Aerosmith. Steven, whose drug use continued, often had to be carried to the stage by a crew member. He was somehow usually capable of making it through a show, although during several concerts he collapsed onstage mid-set. Additionally, the band's kingly traveling style and entourage only served to further distance it from reality. Aerosmith beelined from city to city in a Lear jet, sequestered itself in a centrally located hotel, and left the premises only to travel back and forth to the stadium. A British journalist recalls that it "was the worst example of the superstar syndrome I've ever come across."

Things were made even worse by the drug-fueled rivalry between the group's two creative heavy hitters, Steven, and Joe. The duo had by this point been rechristened "the Toxic Twins" for their willingness to ingest nearly any type of illicit substance. Their rivalry and arguments reached the point where they refused to even sit together in the same limousine. Joe and Steven even sparred during concerts. While working together in close quarters during one performance, Joe punctured Steven's lip with a guitar string. Steven proceeded to retaliate by spitting blood at his band mate. To make matters worse, Steven's new wife, Cyrinda Fox, and Joe's spouse, Elissa Perry, detested each other. Whether onstage or off, there was no peaceful haven for Aerosmith.

Perhaps the seeds of doubt were planted deepest within Joe Perry. Despite his own descent into drug-use and his adjustment to rock 'n' roll success, he seemed to be the most self-effacing in regards to the real price of success: "The more things you do, the more you realize there's no point at which you've made it. . . . I have no illusions about my playing. I did an interview once where the last question was, 'What do you tell somebody who wants to be a good guitar player?' I said, 'I don't know—ask a good guitar player.'"

Following preproduction work at their Boston rehearsal studio in 1979, Aerosmith went into Manhattan's Mediasound Studios to record *Night in the Ruts*. The project was shaky from the start. First, long-time producer and "band member" Jack Douglas had been fired and replaced with Gary Lyons (whose previous clients included Foreigner and Humble Pie). Perhaps more significantly, Steven and Joe's relationship grew even more poisonous. The two leadmen refused to work together in the studio at the same time. As a result, Joe laid down the lion's share of his guitar parts early in the sessions. Steven meanwhile, severely hampered

Steven with daughter Liv, who was born in 1977 but was not aware of who her real father was until the 1990s.

by drug addiction, was taking forever to write the lyrics. Huge blocks of time and money were being wasted in an expensive sound studio from which no album—much less any finished songs—was emerging.

Leber and Krebs decided to send Aerosmith back out on tour to earn back some of the money lost during the recording sessions. But there was another twist. The management team presented Joe with an $80,000 room service bill during a private pre-tour meeting.

They informed him that he was in fact in debt to the Aerosmith organization for a total $100,000; a debt that could be erased if Joe would consider recording a solo album.

Joe, already frustrated with the band's creative slow down, agreed. Steven was livid. He chose, however, not to directly confront Joe. Instead the band went back out on the road without its two leading men speaking to one another. The crisis finally reached its boiling point. A backstage meeting was held among band members and their families following a concert in Cleveland. An ugly showdown erupted. At one point Elissa Perry poured a glass of milk over Tom Hamilton's wife.

In October 1979, Joe told the band to take the guitar tracks he already recorded for *Night in the Ruts* and use them as it wished. He then decided to reenlist producer Jack Douglas and begin work on the first Joe Perry Project album, *Let the Music Do the Talking*. Before starting the album, he made it official—Joe Perry was quitting Aerosmith.

COME TOGETHER

Steven Tyler was hurt and embittered by Joe's departure, but his attitude was emboldened—he was going to complete the new Aerosmith album without Joe. The four remaining band members proceeded to limp forward with *Night in the Ruts*. They hired several guitarists to fill out the arrangements that Joe no longer could. The record was released in November 1979, and to many people's surprise it was impressive. It even featured the departed Joe on the cover. Joe later commented, "[T]here was still a lot of good music in those years. There just wasn't a band together enough to back it up." It is also significant to note that *Night in the Ruts* was the first of Aerosmith's albums not to go platinum.

Aerosmith chose the relatively unknown, Brooklyn-born Jimmy Crespo to take the reigns as lead guitarist for the ensuing tour. It turned out that Crespo wasn't going to be needed for long. After the revamped band played a handful of warm-up gigs and start-off concerts on the east coast, Steven collapsed onstage during a show. The remainder of the tour was canceled.

Things would go from bad to worse for Steven. By 1980

Joe Perry left the band out of frustration with the state of affairs of Aerosmith and began working on his own band, the Joe Perry Project. Soon Brad Whitford would follow suit, leaving Steven Tyler to scramble to find replacements.

he was spending a good portion of his time living in the squalid Gorham Hotel in New York's Hell's Kitchen. Steven used his $20 per day allowance (dispensed by manager David Krebs) to buy heroin. Krebs was reluctant to give him more in fear of an overdose. Steven's mental state deteriorated to the point that he was squeezing toothpaste into the cracks in his walls to keep out the worms and human hands he imagined were pursuing him. In the summer of 1980, under the influence of drugs and alcohol, Steven was nearly killed in a motorcycle accident. He spent the next six months convalescing in the hospital. Unfortunately, instead of improving his drug problem actually worsened. Steven developed a morphine addiction, leading to a dependency on painkillers.

Joe, meanwhile, was traveling in the same direction on a different set of tracks. The Joe Perry Project's initial outing, *Let the Music Do the Talking*, was released in March 1980. Working with vocalist Ralph Morman and producer Douglas, the band had laid down its basic studio tracks in just five days. The album itself was finished in six weeks and came in under budget. The rhythm and blues induced tunes were raw, honest, and energetic, and after suffering the awful stagnation of the Aerosmith recording process, Joe felt invigorated. It was a back-to-basics phase for Joe, and he was happy with the Joe Perry Project playing club gigs and smaller venues rather than arena concerts. Joe proceeded to record *I've Got the Rock 'n' Roll Again* (with Charlie Farren replacing Morman) in 1981 and *Once a Rocker, Always a Rocker* in 1983. Unfortunately, the third album sold only one-sixth—about 40,000 units—the volume of the inaugural *Let the Music Do the Talking*. And, of course, Joe was by this time a confirmed drug addict. His heroin addiction was further aggravated by his tumultuous divorce from Elissa. Joe forfeited most of his money to Elissa in their final settlement and ended up sleeping on the couch of his manager, Tim Collins. Finally, while touring with his band in North Carolina, Joe suffered two drug-induced seizures in one day. This scared him into cleaning up. He said, "I got to thinking a lot about friends of mine who'd died. I was stagnating. I wasn't takin' care of business. I wasn't writing."

Joe wasn't the only one who had left Steven Tyler. While waiting for Steven to recuperate from his accident, Brad Whitford took some time to record his own album, *Whitford/St. Holmes*, with ex-Ted Nugent singer-guitarist Derek St. Holmes. At the time Brad still intended to return to Aerosmith. But when he revisited the old gang in the summer of 1981, he saw a drug-addled Steven and a wayward ship without a creative rudder. Brad decided to make his departure official.

Steven's reaction was one of devout defiance— Who cares? He was going to plow forward no matter what the cost or consequence. He later admitted, "I was so stoned when Brad and Joe jumped ship, I didn't even realize that I was abandoned. I just wanted to keep Aerosmith together." Rick DuFay replaced Brad, and Jimmy Crespo reclaimed Joe's spot. Jack Douglas returned to produce the band's seventh original album, *Rock in a Hard Place*, and did what he could to help clean Steven up. The recording process was an excruciating one, with Steven barely being able to write lyrics. Both he and DuFay drank and took drugs to excess, and drummer Kramer had by now developed a

Jimmy Crespo replaced Joe Perry in 1979, but all was not right with Aerosmith. On Jimmy's first tour with Aerosmith, Steven collapsed onstage, forcing the cancellation of the remainder of the tour.

serious alcohol problem as well. Somehow the album's 10 tracks were completed and released in August 1982. The record was even considered half-decent.

But what was miraculously stitched together during the recording process came wholly undone during the subsequent tour. Rick DuFay became Steven's new party buddy. The band and stage crew developed a set of hand signals to key one another when Steven was on the verge of an onstage collapse. A tour co-manager was given the responsibility of moving the sometimes unconscious performer to and from airports, hotels, and backstage areas. As the road show began to wind down in early 1984, Aerosmith's morale was at an all-time low. The band was surviving, but that's about all. No new songs were being written, and without Perry and Whitford any semblance of cohesion and common purpose had disappeared.

Meanwhile, the Joe Perry Project had stalled. Its record deal with MCA had imploded after the disappointing sales of *Once a Rocker, Always a Rocker*, and despite the fact that Joe had recently written several new songs for Alice Cooper, the professional reality was that Cooper was planning on hiring him as a sideman—not a lead element. It certainly wasn't the same kind of affirmation or swagger he had experienced with ex-comrade-in-arms Steven Tyler in locales from Sunapee, New Hampshire, to Maebashi, Japan.

Little by little, the treacherous ice between Steven and Joe started to thaw. Several members of Aerosmith jammed with Joe during Joe's gig in Salisbury Beach, Massachetts. Joe and Brad showed up at an Aerosmith show in Boston on Valentine's Day in 1984. A month or two later Joe and Steven had a long, cordial phone conversation. Soon the entire band convened—their first congress in over three years. There were still some raw feelings. But there was also a palpable sense of the fellowship's old magic—and the fact that Joe and Steven could work together again. Steven admits, "I hated his guts. I said, 'I never wanted to . . . play on the same stage with you again.' But that's road warp. Time heals all wounds. Joe is nothing without me, and I'm nothing without him. It's like David Lee Roth is nothing without. . . . that's that guitar player's name? Oh, yeah, Eddie Van Halen."

Coming together again was by no means going to be easy. The band was fortunate to have new manager Tim Collins running the show. But there was also its old relationship with Leber and Krebs—and thus a prospective series of lawsuits and financial claims—to contend with. Aerosmith finally geared up to hit the road for its 70-date "Back in the Saddle" comeback tour. The band even adopted Joe's "Let the Music Do the Talking" single from his Joe Perry Project album, a tune that seemed tailor-made for Aerosmith. Once on the circuit, however, it became readily apparent that the band's renewed enthusiasm wouldn't be enough to bury its destructive behavior. In Springfield, Illinois, Steven downed a few drinks (on top of the pills he was popping) before going onstage. He proceeded to stumble through an embarrassing, nearly incoherent performance. A fan grabbed his scarf, and Steven fell off the stage. The band, disgusted, walked off the stage in protest.

The Springfield debacle was an unfortunate, but necessary, setback. Whereas the band wasn't ready to confront its substance abuse problems, it did understand what had to happen with its music. In 1985, Aerosmith switched record labels, beginning an exciting new relationship with Geffen Records. Then—with John Kalodner starting his tenure as the band's A&R rep— Aerosmith went into Fantasy Studios in Berkeley, California, to record *Done With Mirrors*, its first original album in six years. Released in 1985, *Done With Mirrors* was engineered to be the group's comeback bonanza. It was met, however, with a lackluster reception; the album failed to go even gold. Like the humiliating incident in Springfield, *Done With Mirrors'* poor performance offered itself up as a cautionary tale. The old Aerosmith had disappeared from the music scene for more than half a decade. The rock world and the marketplace had changed. New young bands like Motley Crue and Twisted Sister had stepped into the vacuum. They were not only trumping Aerosmith at its own game— loud and brash rock 'n' roll with attitude to spare—but had spurred a new generation of teenagers into record stores and concert halls. It was one thing for Aerosmith to be romantic about reuniting. It was another to reclaim the effort and dedication necessary to be taken seriously again.

The band was helped along by the unexpected smash success of Run-DMC's rap reworking of "Walk This Way" in 1986. Whereas the fusion of two such different groups might at first seem remarkable, it turned out that the heavy metal sound had long been a favorite of Run-DMC. The commercial timing for black rap meeting white rock couldn't have been better; both forms were struggling to break free from their niches and attract a wider, more diverse audience. Run-DMC asked Aerosmith to both participate in the recording studio and with the accompanying music video. Steven and Joe's dynamic performances in that video went a long way toward ushering Aerosmith back into the mainstream. The new "Walk This Way" became a number four single in the United States and a number eight in England.

There was one hitch, however. Drugs. Producer Rick Rubin was one of the masterminds of the new rock-rap fusion. He was also an old

Aerosmith's career was resurrected when Run-DMC did a rap version of "Walk This Way." Aerosmith even appeared in the video as well as contributing music to the song.

Aerosmith fan and hung out with Joe and Steven while recording "Walk This Way." Rubin expressed an interest in producing Aerosmith's next album, and the guys were equally enthused—they were quite literally flying high. Joe recalls, "We figured we'd go into the studio with him and record a song one night. I had methadone in one pocket, some blow in one pocket, some pills in another pocket, and a bottle of rum. . . . The next day we listened to the tape and I was just embarrassed about how we must have acted. And the song sucked. It was time for a major change. For me, and for everyone else in the band."

Aerosmith had talked about change before; it had never happened. Finally manager Tim Collins—with the full weight of Geffen Records behind him—gave the band an ultimatum; sobriety or failure. If the choice was going to be option number two, the band's new business partners wouldn't stick around to clean up the mess.

6

BLUE SKY

In 1986, Tim checked the entire band into a rehab center known as the Caron Foundation. Aerosmith embarked upon a brutal—yet ultimately effective—12-step program. Nothing less than brutal would have been enough to uproot a drug and alcohol problem that reached back nearly 20 years. "We were sick and tired of feeling sick and tired," remembers Joe. There were other motivations as well. Joe was now married to his second wife, Billie, who had just given birth to their son, Anthony (the couple had two other children—Adrian from Joe's first marriage and Aaron from Billie's first). All channels— professional, creative, and personal—were converging into the one main riverbed of getting healthy. Steven ruminates in regards to cleaning up: "Tell [everyone] how hard it is, how beautiful it is. I tell them there's a whole world of music out there, and they're living in a cave with a boulder at the door, and the boulder is drugs. You kick the boulder out of the way, you can go in and out, invite your friends in." In the documentary film, *The Decline of Western Civilization: The Heavy Metal Years*, Joe and Steven were asked whether they could still make great music without drugs. At the time (1987) they had been clean and sober for 11 months. Replied Steven, "Positively. Better, too."

Steven Tyler and Joey Kramer with the Aerosmith-sponsored "Screaming Demon" racecar driven by Jeff Ward—an apt partnership considering the fast living that Aerosmith has done in the past.

Aerosmith and Collins returned to the studio with Canadian producer, Bruce Fairbairn, in 1986. The *Permanent Vacation* album was recorded at Little Mountain Sound in Vancouver. Two major advancements were evident. First, the band was clean, and the tardiness, bitterness, and near-chaos that plagued earlier recording sessions had dissipated (the exceptions to the rule were Tom Hamilton and Joey Kramer; Joey would continue to wrestle with alcohol dependence through the creation of *Nine Lives*, when he suffered a breakdown). Second, A&R rep John Kalodner introduced Steven and Joe to a selection of outside writers and song doctors, including Desmond Child, Jim Vallance, and Holly Knight. The songwriters had written tunes for hit recording artists like Kiss, Bon Jovi, and Bryan Adams, and Kalodner felt that they might have a better understanding of the contemporary marketplace. The collaboration was a significant adjustment for Steven and Joe, who were used to being the sole authors of the Aerosmith repertoire. In addition, the pair was still trying to formulate a way of creating and playing music without drug use— the question was now how they were going to accomplish this while simultaneously listening to and absorbing other people's ideas. The challenge was greater than producing a hit single. It was to create a sound and direction that unified the band.

The song-doctors had a hand in writing 7 of *Permanent Vacation*'s 11 original compositions, and their contributions were a perfectly organic complement to Aerosmith's own reinvigorated approach. The record was released in August 1987 and was an absolute triumph; the real Aerosmith comeback album. *Permanent Vacation* went triple-platinum and produced three smash hit singles—"Angel," "Dude (Looks Like a Lady)," and "Rag Doll." Kalodner also hooked up the band with video director, Marty Callner. He directed music videos for each of the hit singles, and their popularity catapulted the band solidly into the contemporary MTV arena.

The 10-month concert tour promoting *Permanent Vacation* not only brought Aerosmith back into the upper echelon of the rock 'n' roll world, it sparked a critical appreciation that had always eluded the band. *Newsday* magazine gave the group a positive review. *Billboard* magazine and newspapers such as the *Boston Globe* and *Atlanta Constitution* offered nods of respect. Bit by bit, the band's rededication was paying off.

Pump was released in 1989 and picked up where *Permanent Vacation* left off. By this juncture Tom Hamilton had embraced sobriety, and his renewed creativity helped energize the recording sessions. The musicians not only introduced a batch of tight, aggressive, and commercial new songs, they were being sparked in ways they hadn't known since the band's inception. *Pump's* intriguing musical interludes—including tribal chants and exotic instrumental snippets—were motivated by Izzy Stradlin's esoteric ethnic music tapes. (Stradlin and Guns N' Roses had headlined the third leg of the *Permanent Vacation* tour.) Joe got the idea for "Don't Get Mad" after going home and listening to "Rag Doll" backwards. "The chords just hit me," he says. Steven wrote the tune's lyrics the very next day. Additionally, "Janie's Got a Gun" is one of the few Aerosmith songs that confronts a social issue or crisis. Steven had just read a *Time* magazine article about teenage suicide. The article examined young adults who were in and out of rehab because of parental abuse and molestation.

The release of *Pump* cemented Aerosmith's reputation as a rock band that was still making hits and rocking as hard as they ever did, as the band won numerous awards and enjoyed a highly successful tour.

Remembers Hamilton, "Steven came in and played 'Janie's Got a Gun' one day at rehearsal, and we all just kind of stood there. It was like a visit from the gods. There was something really amazing happening in that room." Not surprisingly, next to "Dream On," "Janie's Got a Gun" is the Aerosmith song that garners the most fan mail.

By the time the *Pump* concert circuit had wound down, Aerosmith was second to only the Rolling Stones in cumulative U.S. tour receipts. The album itself sold more than four million copies. In September 1990, Aerosmith won three MTV Video Music Awards. It subsequently captured a Grammy award for "Janie's Got a Gun" for Best Rock Performance. And a *Rolling Stone* Reader's Poll listed the quintet as Best American Band. If there had been any residual doubt about Aerosmith's talent, adaptability, and determination, it had been summarily extinguished.

The band's next original album for Geffen was *Get a Grip*. The recording, supervised by Bruce Fairbairn, ran into a number of difficulties. At one point Kalodner, feeling that the material wasn't strong enough, actually walked into a session at A&M Studios in Los Angeles and pulled the plug. Ultimately, with the help of outside songwriters like Vallance, Richie Supa, and Lenny Kravitz (the R&B laced "Line Up"), *Get a Grip* was released in 1993. The album sold five million units domestically and another five million abroad, and was the band's first album to reach number one on the *Billboard* 200. And with the vision of director Marty Callner, the music videos for "Livin' on the Edge," "Crazy," and "Amazing" made a huge splash on MTV. In a prophetic act of casting, "Crazy" introduced Steven's daughter, Liv Tyler, as a budding nymphet. Liv would pay her dad back in spades five years down the road with a little movie named *Armageddon*.

Aerosmith had made huge, undeniable strides. But beneath the surface, tensions—and Joey Kramer's alcoholism—still lingered. The band's challenge of keeping its focus—and friendships—strong was a formidable one. Says Kramer, "You could search the ends of the earth and I don't think you could find five more different guys." Ultimately, Aerosmith consulted addiction specialist Steven Chatoff in 1996. Chatoff was at the time the director of a Port Hueneme rehabilitation center. He was a successful graduate of an Alcoholics Anonymous 12-step program and specialized in helping music and entertainment artists confront the pressures and temptations of success. Whereas Aerosmith's drug indulgences were behind them, the band decided to fly in from

Boston for two weeks of conflict negotiation. Joe said, "They convinced us to stay there and stay focused, and besides it would be a good example for the thirty-day people who were there trying to get sober."

The tumultuous and painful sessions ended in a conclusion—that long-time manager Tim Collins was actually trying to tear the band members apart. One of Tim's ploys was leaking the rumor that Steven was taking drugs again. Steven was incensed. On one hand he realized he was an easy target. On the other, he knew how hard he had worked to get sober. Steven recalls, "I mean, my eight-year-old daughter came to me and said, 'My best friend can't come to my first sleep-over because her daddy says you're on drugs. What are drugs, Daddy?' How do you think that made me feel?"

Tim was fired. New York-based Wendy Laister was hired. The band's next studio album (it had left Geffen Records and returned to Columbia), ironically their thirteenth, was the aptly named *Nine Lives*. Released in 1997, the album went double-platinum almost immediately. But its success was a mere taste of what was to come; the popularity of the singles "Falling in Love (Is Hard on the Knees)" and "Pink" (the music video featured the band in full cross-dressing glory) were an appetizer for a regal main course. Aerosmith released *A Little South of Sanity*, a double-disc live CD in 1998. Within two weeks the album sold one and a half million units in Japan alone. And then came *Armageddon*. Aerosmith contributed four songs to the film, which eventually became the top-grossing movie of 1998. "I Don't Want to Miss a Thing" (written by Diane Warren; she had written hit singles for Toni Braxton, Celine Dion, and Trisha Yearwood) became Aerosmith's first-ever

number one single. And then the band was invited to the White House. And then to Cape Canaveral for the space shuttle launch. . . . Aerosmith was flying as high as it possibly could. Blue sky was all around; and the dark clouds of drugs and alcohol nowhere in sight.

On March 26, 1998, Steven Tyler turned 50 years old. Joe Perry was 48. In 2001 Aerosmith released its 14th studio CD, *Just Push Play*. The band, together for 31 years, was still pushing play and finding a way to make its music and partnership matter. Concludes Joe Perry, "There are certainly better musicians than all of us out there, but it takes more than musicianship to be in a band. I look at those guys [in Aerosmith], and they're like time travelers with me. They've been through every black hole that I have. . . . Maybe we're here to show people that it can be done. You can come out of the depths and survive with pride. And that's a message that we're carrying to people."

Aerosmith continues to amaze and delight music fans today. They have survived situations that should have rightfully killed them years ago, if not split up the band altogether. But not only have they survived to continue playing and recording, but were finally recognized as legends in their own right when they were inducted into the Rock and Roll Hall of Fame in 2001.

CHRONOLOGY

1948	Steven Tyler (birth name Steven Tallarico) born on March 26 in New York City
1950	Joey Kramer born on June 21 in New York City; Joe Perry born on September 10 in Lawrence, Mass.
1951	Tom Hamilton born on Dec. 31 in New York City
1952	Brad Whitford born on Feb. 23 in Colorado Springs, Colorado
1970	Aerosmith debuts at Nimpoc Regional High School in Hopkinton, Mass.
1973	Aerosmith releases its first album, *Aerosmith*, on the Columbia Records label
1974	Aerosmith makes first national television appearance on NBC's *Midnight Special*
1975	Columbia Records releases *Toys In The Attic* (includes hit single "Walk This Way")
1976	"Dream On" (rereleased from first album) becomes band's first Top 10 single
1978	Aerosmith makes its silver screen debut in the film *Sgt. Pepper's Lonely Hearts Club Band*
1979	Joe Perry leaves the band
1980	The Joe Perry Project releases its first album, *Let The Music Do The Talking*
1981	Brad Whitford leaves Aerosmith
1984	Aerosmith's original line-up reunites
1986	Run-DMC covers Aerosmith's "Walk This Way"; Aerosmith contributes to both studio work and accompanying music video; Band checks into rehabilitation center to tackle its legacy of substance abuse

1989   *Pump* released; includes "Janie's Got A Gun," which becomes a No. 4 single

1996   The band, still wrestling with internecine rivalries and abuse difficulties, consults with addiction specialist Steven Chatoff

1998   Single "I Don't Want To Miss A Thing" from the movie *Armageddon* becomes the band's first-ever No. 1 single

2001   Aerosmith is voted into the Rock and Roll Hall of Fame

ACCOMPLISHMENTS

Discography

1973	*Aerosmith*
1974	*Get Your Wings*
1975	*Toys in the Attic*
1976	*Rocks*
1977	*Draw the Line*
1978	*Live Bootleg*
1979	*Night in the Ruts*
1980	*Greatest Hits*
1982	*Rock in a Hard Place*
1985	*Done with Mirrors* *Classics Live*
1987	*Classics Live 2* *Permanent Vacation*
1988	*Gems*
1989	*Pump*
1991	*Pandora's Box*
1993	*Get a Grip*
1994	*Big Ones* *Box of Fire*
1997	*Nine Lives*
1998	*A Little South of Sanity*
2001	*Just Push Play* *Young Lust: The Aerosmith Anthology—The Geffen Years*

AWARDS

1988	MTV Music Award—Best Group Video for "Dude Looks Like A Lady"
	Best Stage Performance in a Video for "Dude Looks Like a Lady"
1990	MTV Music Award—Best Metal/Hard Rock Video for "Janie's Got A Gun"
	Viewers Choice Award for "Janie's Got A Gun"
	Grammy Award for "Janie's Got A Gun"—Best Rock Performance by a Duo or Group With Vocal
	MTV Music Award—Best Metal/Hard Rock Video for "The Other Side"
1991	Voted into the Boston Garden Hall of Fame
1993	MTV Music Award—Viewers Choice for "Livin' On The Edge"
	Grammy Award for "Livin' On The Edge"—Best Rock Performance by a Duo or Group With Vocal
1994	MTV Music Award—Best Video for "Cryin'"
	Best Group Video for "Cryin'"
	Viewers Choice for "Cryin'"
	Grammy Award for "Crazy"—Best Rock Performance by a Duo or Group With Vocal
1997	MTV Music Award—"Falling In Love (Is Hard On The Knees)"
1998	Grammy Award for "Pink"—Best Rock Performance by a Duo or Group With Vocal
1999	Billboard Music Association Award—"Artist Achievement Award"
2001	Inducted into Rock and Roll Hall of Fame

FURTHER READING

Aerosmith and Davis, Stephen. *Walk This Way: The Autobiography of Aerosmith*. New York: William Morrow and Company, 1999.

Foxe-Tyler, Cyrinda. *Dream On: Livin' on the Edge with Steven Tyler and Aerosmith*. New York: Berkley Books, 2000.

Huxley, Martin. *Aerosmith: The Fall and the Rise of Rock's Greatest Band*. New York: St. Martin's Press, 1995.

ABOUT THE AUTHOR

ERIK KEITH ANJOU was born in the Philadelphia area. After graduating from the William Penn Charter School in Germantown, he was fortunate to jump the accelerated train to higher education, having attended Middlebury College (B.A.), Northwestern University (M.A.) and the American Film Institute's Center for Advanced Film Studies (Directing Program). Erik has sustained a foothold across a broad range of filmic and literary pursuits. He has written and directed several feature and documentary films. Most recently, he completed his first novel. Erik currently resides in New York City and revisits Philadelphia often to play with his nieces, Eliza Sophie and Madeleine Amelia, and root on the Flyers.

INDEX